Is There a Way
Through Suffering?

Is There a Way Through Suffering?

Pat Lynch

DARTON, LONGMAN AND TODD
LONDON

First published in 1992 by
Darton, Longman and Todd Ltd
89 Lillie Road, London SW6 1UD

© 1992 Pat Lynch

ISBN 0–232–51964–1

A catalogue record for this book is available
from the British Library

The Scripture quotations are taken from the
Jerusalem Bible, published and copyright 1966, 1967 and 1968, by
Darton, Longman and Todd Ltd and Doubleday & Co Inc
and used by permission of the publishers

Cover: *Weeping Woman* (1937) by Pablo Picasso.
The Tate Gallery, London. © DACS.

Phototypeset in 10/11½ pt Trump by Intype, London
Printed and bound in Great Britain
at the University Press, Cambridge

Contents

I dedicate this work to the many people
who have shared their life stories with me
making my life richer
and more profound.

Introduction

◆━━━➤

THE WRITINGS OF THE BIBLE – the Scriptures – are the Word of God. They are of supreme importance to all Christians and to all who wish to know and understand the meaning of Christianity. The Bible should be in every Christian home. Every aspect of Christian life and worship should reflect in some way what God says to his people. Catholics have not always been very good at reading and studying the Bible. In 1965 during the Second Vatican Council a document on Scripture as the Word of God (*Dei Verbum*) was published. This has had a marked effect in laying the foundations for an official programme of encouragement to Catholics to make the Bible central to their lives.

Much has happened since then. Every public act of worship has its reading from Scripture. Scripture (both Old and New Testaments) has a significant place in all religious education programmes, whether for adults or for children. The lectionary for the readings at daily and Sunday Mass covers a large amount of Scripture during its three-year cycle. Familiar acts of devotion like the Rosary and the Stations of the Cross have become far more scripturally based.

The positive value of this is obvious enough. But it has also meant that many Catholics have been thrown in at the deep end. They are a little like the Ethiopian in his carriage on the way home from Jerusalem who was reading some Scripture. Philip the Deacon heard him and asked him if he understood what he was reading. 'How can I', the man said, 'unless I have someone to guide me?' (Acts 8:26–40). Most of us do need help if we are to understand what we are reading. It is not that the language of Scripture is particularly difficult; it is rather that its context is so often unfamiliar.

I warmly welcome this series of *Scripture for Living*. Its particular value is that it helps us to see how Scripture is relevant to our daily lives. There are many other books for scholars. This series is for ordinary Christians who treasure Scripture, know for certain that it is of fundamental importance, but who are not sure how to make sense of what they read or how to relate it to their daily lives and experiences.

The pattern of the series is story, bible passage, commentary, reflection and prayer. There is a natural progression in this. The writings in the Bible (which form a whole library really) are about people trying to recognise God in their lives. So the context is just everyday life – the stuff of story. Story leads on naturally to Scripture because Scripture is itself about life in all its variety. So it speaks of love and hate, success and failure, death and resurrection; almost every imaginable human failing and strength finds place in it, simply because it is about real people. The commentary is an aid to understanding. Then, since the ultimate purpose of Scripture is to lead people closer to God, the text finishes with a prayer which ties together what has gone before and shows how our daily lives can be enriched.

The series is ideal for use in groups as well as by individuals. I wish it every success.

+ DAVID KONSTANT
Bishop of Leeds

Preface

THIS BOOK IS OFFERED to try to help people see a way through the many problems and difficulties facing them. It has developed out of my encounters with people, both in my former pastoral role as a parish priest and in my present work as a Catholic evangelist.

There is a body of opinion which says discussion of Scripture should be left to those who are specialists in the field, but that rule is broken by this book. My work is bound to have the imperfections that inevitably result when the general practitioner intrudes within the province of the specialist. However, my interpretation of Scripture is in no way an attempt to refute arguments or define dogma in Christian practice – it is merely an attempt to offer help from the Bible to people who are experiencing pain and suffering in their lives.

The Scripture scholars have not gone on strike, nor have they overlooked the importance of the issues dealt with in this book. If they were asked, perhaps many of them would reply that no more momentous question confronts them than that of seeing how the Scriptures relate to real life problems. But I am writing simply out of my own experience. I feel that there is a great need among ordinary people to know that their suffering can find some relief in the Bible. We can find comfort and solace from knowing that many others have experienced the same or similar difficulties as ourselves – the Scriptures are full of pain and suffering and tell us how men and women have coped with it in their lives.

As an evangelist it is my privilege to meet thousands of people from different backgrounds, nations and cultures. Something they all have in common is pain – the pain of being human. People do not live detached, unthinking lives; we are constantly asking questions. What is it all about? Is there a God? If there is a God, does he really care? How can he love me in the midst of my sin and pain? There are no easy answers to the question of suffering. Often all I can do is empathise with the people who share their problems and doubts with me. I must confess that I have a great love for people, especially when they are down or depressed. I feel honoured when they share with me their innermost selves.

I have listened to many stories throughout my life, and I have learned something of the journey each person has to make. We sometimes sat in silence, entering into the pain, sharing the sadness without needing words. I learned about the longing of people's hearts, the loneliness of their lives, their need for love and affirmation. I heard of dreams that were shattered, visions unfulfilled, hopes disappearing. I was told of isolation and bitterness, joy and laughter that turned stale. I felt the budding of new life in the searching of each soul and could see people's dignity as they trod their own muddy and twisted path. It seems that often all we have to hold onto is the hope that life springs from death and light from darkness. One truth kept coming back to me as I wrote this book: God is always saying, 'Love each other and take the hand of my suffering people'. I pray that as you read the stories which follow you will realise that in pain which is shared God can rise and live within you.

I believe that all books have many authors, and that is especially true of *Is There a Way Through Suffering?* I feel as if I have been no more than the pen through which others have written. I would like to express my deepest thanks to all the people whose stories are told in this work. It was they who gave me permission to share their struggles so that others could be helped.

The administrator of the Sion Community, Mrs

Audrey Gibbs, and its secretary, Mrs Frances Landreth, somehow deciphered my writing and transferred it into a meaningful typescript. I am grateful to them for their patience and expertise, especially in putting up with my last-minute changes.

I would like also to thank all the members of the Sion Community for bearing with me as I wrote this book and for taking on some of my work load so that the manuscript could be completed on schedule.

Special thanks go to Morag Reeve and Sharon Milne, my editors at Darton, Longman and Todd, who have given me constant support and encouragement and through their suggestions have brought order to this book.

If, despite all its imperfections, *Is There a Way Through Suffering?* helps even one person to make contact with the Word of God and enables them to see how it relates to real life, then it will have fully achieved its aim.

PAT LYNCH

Why Me?

◆──────◆

WHEN I WAS A YOUNG PRIEST starting out in my vocation, I was called to the local city hospital one night to help a family who had suffered an unexpected tragedy. As I entered the hospital, I was a bit cocky, eager to put into practice all that I had learned. I know this is an attitude which tempts all of us at times, but how quickly one's preconceptions can be shattered. Facing me in the corridor was a middle-aged couple, heartbroken and distressed. The woman's voice shook as she told me her son was dead, that he had taken an overdose.

I longed to comfort them to help them make sense of a senseless situation. I expected their anger and resentment against God and society, but instead the woman said, 'We know that God is good – but why us, Lord?' I couldn't reply. Instead I held them both in my arms. As it turned out, the couple coped with the tragedy and went on to help others in the same situation. Yet long afterwards the words 'Why us, Lord?' kept coming back to me.

When we come up against difficult and disturbing questions that defy answers we tend to push them aside or bury them, but years later they resurrect themselves and haunt us, coming to the forefront of our minds when we are lonely, isolated or depressed.

One such occasion for me was August 1987. I had been preaching in New Orleans. Many people long to see other countries and have new experiences, but sometimes it can be lonely. I was on board a plane bound for Nashville, after having been away from home for two months. I had pleasant memories of speaking to and meeting lots of people and seeing them respond to God's love, but now I was alone with my own thoughts and feelings. As I made my way into the terminal building in Nashville, music was being played over the tannoy system. Suddenly, the lyrics of a song pierced my ears: 'Why me, Lord, what did I ever do to deserve such as this?'. The song seemed to be blaring out just for me. Having made my way to a corner seat, I found myself reliving a tragedy that had occurred in my own life.

My mind went back several years to a wintry evening in 1982. I had had a busy day and decided to visit a very dear family who were long-standing friends of mine. Philip and Frances were happily married with two boys and another child on the way. I turned up on their doorstep and we spent a few hours catching up on things. After a while, Philip said he had to go into town to get some things they needed from the store. I handed him the keys of my car, which he accepted.

Frances and I resumed our conversation and became almost oblivious of time. Philip's trip should have taken less than half an hour, but eventually I looked at my watch to realise that he had been gone for an hour and a half. Knowing he was an extrovert, I reassured myself that he had met someone and started chatting, but at the back of my mind I felt anxious that something was wrong. Suddenly the front door opened and Richard, Philip's brother, came in. 'There's been an accident', he said. 'Philip has been killed.'

What had been a great evening had become a nightmare. I remembered my two friends at the hospital all those years ago; now tragedy had entered my own life. I was the one left asking, 'Why me, Lord?' I had ministered to others in death; now it was my turn.

In the following days, I felt the deep love and compassion of others, and through it all, prayer was my constant sustenance. At times of tragedy we tend to overlook our own feelings because of the swift nature of events — so many things have to be done that the flood of action can carry us along. I was dreading the funeral as I sat down with the family to prepare the service. I had just lost a good friend. Now, piled on top of my grief, was the prospect of having to face a large congregation. Could I see it all through without breaking down in tears?

I made my way to my bible to seek a relevant passage in the life of Jesus where he experienced similar pains of loss and grief. I wanted to open a window of hope for Frances, the family and the people who would attend the funeral service. I realised that every view of where we are and what we hope for is personal. Somehow I had to show that there was hope in what appeared to be a point-less loss of life. The passage that seemed most relevant for the occasion was the resurrection of Lazarus.

There was a man named Lazarus who lived in the village of Bethany with the two sisters, Mary and Martha, and he was ill. – It was the same Mary, the sister of the sick man Lazarus, who anointed the Lord with ointment and wiped his feet with her hair. The sisters sent this message to Jesus, 'Lord, the man you love is ill' . . .

On arriving, Jesus found that Lazarus had been in the tomb for four days already. Bethany is only about two miles from Jerusalem, and many Jews had come to Martha and Mary to sympathise with them over their brother. When Martha heard that Jesus had come she went to meet him. Mary remained sitting in the house. Martha said to Jesus, 'If you had been here, my brother would not have died, but I know that, even now, what-ever you ask of God, he will grant you'. 'Your brother' said Jesus to her 'will rise again.' Martha said, 'I know he will rise again at the resurrection on the last day'. Jesus said:

'I am the resurrection.
If anyone believes in me, even though he dies he will
   live,
and whoever lives and believes in me

will never die.
Do you believe this?'

'Yes Lord,' she said 'I believe that you are the Christ, the Son of God, the one who was to come into this world.'

When she had said this, she went and called her sister Mary, saying in a low voice, 'The Master is here and wants to see you'. Hearing this, Mary got up quickly and went to him. Jesus had not yet come into the village; he was still at the place where Martha had met him. When the Jews who were in the house sympathising with Mary saw her get up so quickly and go out, they followed her, thinking that she was going to the tomb to weep there.

Mary went to Jesus, and as soon as she saw him she threw herself at his feet, saying, 'Lord, if you had been here, my brother would not have died'. At the sight of her tears, and those of the Jews who followed her, Jesus said in great distress, with a sigh that came straight from the heart, 'Where have you put him?' They said, 'Lord, come and see'. Jesus wept; and the Jews said, 'See how much he loved him!' But there were some who remarked, 'He opened the eyes of the blind man, could he not have prevented this man's death?' Still sighing, Jesus reached the tomb: it was a cave with a stone to close the opening. Jesus said, 'Take the stone away'. Martha said to him, 'Lord, by now he will smell; this is the fourth day'. Jesus replied, 'Have I not told you that if you believe you will see the glory of God?' So they took away the stone. Then Jesus lifted up his eyes and said:

'Father, I thank you for hearing my prayer.
I knew indeed that you always hear me,
but I speak
for the sake of all these who stand round me,
so that they may believe it was you who sent me.'

When he had said this, he cried in a loud voice, 'Lazarus, here! Come out!' The dead man came out, his feet and hands bound with bands of stuff and a cloth round his face. Jesus said to them, 'Unbind him, let him go free'.

(John 11:1–3; 17–44)

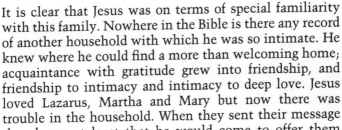

It is clear that Jesus was on terms of special familiarity with this family. Nowhere in the Bible is there any record of another household with which he was so intimate. He knew where he could find a more than welcoming home; acquaintance with gratitude grew into friendship, and friendship to intimacy and intimacy to deep love. Jesus loved Lazarus, Martha and Mary but now there was trouble in the household. When they sent their message they knew at least that he would come to offer them comfort. After Lazarus' death, friends would have come in numbers so that by the time Jesus arrived the house would have been full. Martha and Mary would have been there seeing to their friends, offering them refreshments and showing gratitude for their messages of condolence. There doesn't seem to have been any resentment towards Jesus for not having come immediately. They loved him and trusted him.

When they heard of his arrival. Martha hurried down the road to meet him. Jesus' disciples would have known her. They knew her sorrow and were only too willing to admit her to where she would most certainly find consolation. Whatever else they had learned from the Master they would have remembered the words: 'Come to me all who labour and are overburdened, and I will give you rest' (Matthew 11:28). When Martha finally met Jesus she had only one thought: 'If you had been here this would not have happened'. She immediately expressed her faith in Jesus; she knew that he was a friend and that in the end, now that he was near, all would be well. Almost without thinking she blurts out, 'I know whatever you ask of God he will grant you'. Jesus must have remembered all the things she had done for him in the past. Now it was his turn to help her. He said to her, 'Your brother will rise.' She could not understand:

how could she? Dead men do not rise; even Jesus had not
raised to life a body that had been dead and buried.
Martha thought he must be speaking about the next life,
of the great resurrection. 'I know he will rise on the
last day', she said. But Jesus' reply was one of authority,
compelling faith, even though what he said was shrouded
in mystery. For a moment he seems to play with words,
above all with the word 'life', telling Martha 'I am the
resurrection. If anyone believes in me he will live'. What
could poor Martha make of all this? Others more learned
or more experienced in Jesus' teachings might have understood better. All Martha knew was that she trusted him.

I am afraid that, like Martha, I was running around
asking questions and searching for answers in the midst
of my own tragedy, but what of Philip's wife, Frances?
Was Frances behaving a bit like Mary in the story,
unseen, unheard, yet still in the depths of anxiety?

Mary must have been experiencing the disappoint-
ment, the mourning, the emptiness. Her nature meant,
she had taken the loss of her brother more deeply to
heart. Maybe her independent nature defied all comfort.
Could the message of this story speak to Frances? Martha
went to fetch Mary. When Mary knew that Jesus had
come the words acted like magic. Mary had always been
made to feel like a queen, born to command and lead,
who could do nothing ignobly. She ran to Jesus and said,
'If you had been here my brother would not have died.'
Jesus did not try her as he had tried her sister – he saw
her tears which caused him to weep too. He was a true
friend, identifying with the situation. Could Frances feel
God's presence in the midst of her pain? She had known
the comfort and consolation of God in the past: could
this knowledge sustain her now?

Despite my feeling that somewhere in the midst of it
all was the hand of God, there was a bargaining process
going on. If I hadn't gone to their home that evening . . .
if I hadn't offered the keys to my car, would it all have
been different? I know that similar sentiments are constantly on the lips of many people in these circum-

stances. I was consoled to find the same bargaining process in the bible story. Lazarus had died. Martha approached Jesus who told her, 'I am the resurrection'. In these short lines Martha is moved from the past to the future tense: Jesus brings her back to the present tense with the words 'I am'. This made me realise that in every conceivable situation Jesus 'is'. Could we find comfort in this?

When the day of Philip's funeral arrived, it was a bit like a thief in the night: it crept up on me. Somehow when we are powerless our predicament is a prime breeding ground for the apparently impossible. How was I going to minister on this day? How would the family deal with it? I pondered and prayed deeply upon the words, 'I am the resurrection'. Here, for me history touched mystery, time upon eternity. Philip was dead. We were to bury him, but somehow he lived with the Father.

Frances and I have had lots of time to talk since the funeral. We still feel the pain of loss, but because of Jesus' words there is hope in the midst of despair, loss and tragedy. We are slaves to time, relationships, humanity, the world, to mention but a few, yet we know that there is always hope, whose eternal name is Christ, and who has been there before us.

FOR REFLECTION

1. If you have experienced personal tragedy in your life, were you able to see any point in it at the time?
2. What do you feel sustained you through your tragedy?
3. Do you really appreciate that Jesus has been there before us and can identify with our pain and suffering?
4. In what way is Jesus the resurrection and the life for you?

PRAYER

O Lord, into your hands I give my spirit and the spirit of
all those whom I love. I commend to you all those who
have died, those who are fearful of death or fearful of life.
I commend to you all those who fear change, especially
the change of circumstances that death brings about.

Why Us?

◆——◆

MY TIME WITH MY MEMORIES was up. My flight was being called over the tannoy system, and I had to bid farewell to Nashville and try to put aside my own painful memories for a while. It was late afternoon and the sun was hot; I noticed the grass was brown and the flowers peppered with fine dust as I boarded the aircraft.

To get to my seat I had to scramble over an elderly couple and although I was determined to fall asleep, I was distracted by their lively conversation. Soon I felt I had to introduce myself.

Their names were Kate and David. They made an attractive couple, and seemed to complement each other perfectly. The man was tall, stately and gentle; the woman small, quick and vivacious. You could tell they loved each other.

As soon as he started chatting it was if we were old friends, but I noticed their discomfort when I revealed that I was a Catholic priest. I knew something was wrong but didn't know what it could be or what I could do about it. Why these sudden uncomfortable silences? David was the one who finally broke the uneasiness. 'May we share with you, Father?' he asked without warning. His face was white as he tried to smile, and I noticed Kate was shaking.

'Yes, of course', I replied. 'Go ahead.'

Kate and David's story was one of pain and suffering, of guilt and self-condemnation.

They told me they were both Catholics and had been

married for forty-five years. They had struggled to bring up a large family through troubled times and now had several grandchildren. They described their family as close-knit and loving. Both were of Irish descent and they had received a good Catholic education which they had tried to pass on to their children. Their faith had always been central to their lives. But now as they looked back over the years they were asking where they had 'gone wrong'.

Like so many other Catholic parents they were distressed because almost all their children had given up the practice of their faith. It is a story I have often heard. But everyone's story is unique and there is something new and fresh when it is honestly shared by two very passionate parents.

David and Kate had tried to talk through the issue with their children. 'We met with a brick wall', they told me. Eventually after a friendly family get-together at which one son had made a disparaging remark about the Bible, they decided to open up the subject by writing a letter and sending a copy to each member of the family. David pulled from his pocket a ragged piece of paper, which he handed to me hesitantly.

'Dear Sons and Daughters', it began. 'Your mother and I wanted to do this because of the comment made by Steve when we last saw you all.

Steve asked us, 'Surely you don't believe all that stuff in the Bible? Surely you can't believe all the Church has to say?' We find it difficult to talk about our faith with you all except on a superficial level. All we want to share with you is the love that God has shown us. It hasn't always been easy but somehow we know that God is always with us guiding us, even when we aren't listening. We love you all so much that we want to share this wonderful truth with you.

Although the Catholic Church as an institution has, at one time or another, demonstrated all the faults of which human beings can be guilty, it has also served to nurture the relationship of millions of people with God. Surely no one should be completely rejected because of their shortcomings?

Our belief is that God communicated himself to us on our own level by becoming human. That is the significance of Jesus. His life is an understanding of what life should be. The Bible is an account of how God has acted in the lives of humans, particularly in sending his son. Your mother and I have come to accept that Jesus is real. He is a living person who is with us constantly, and our prayer for you all is that you have the same experience of him.'

Kate and David's letter showed a deep concern for the family and was a passionate plea to them to rethink their lives. It was obvious they realised that no human reasoning and no logical arguments can give a person faith: faith is the domain of God and it is a gift. As David asked at the end of his letter, 'Can an experience shared by millions be rejected as a myth merely because it doesn't fit in with modern day thinking and cannot be submitted to tests?'

Kate and David seemed pleased that I had taken the trouble to read their letter. After I handed it back, there followed one of those long silences which seem neverending. They seemed to expect me to come up with an answer. Is there an answer? I thought to myself. Apprehensively, I took out my bible, wondering what their reactions would be.

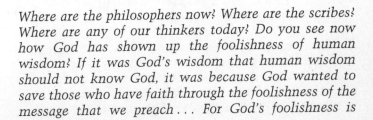

Where are the philosophers now? Where are the scribes? Where are any of our thinkers today? Do you see now how God has shown up the foolishness of human wisdom? If it was God's wisdom that human wisdom should not know God, it was because God wanted to save those who have faith through the foolishness of the message that we preach ... For God's foolishness is

wiser than human wisdom, and God's weakness is stronger than human strength.

(1 Corinthians 1:20–1;25)

David and Kate seemed to be in a bewildered state when I finished reading this passage. I felt that I had hurt them in some way. 'It is amazing', David said at last, 'that you quoted that passage, because it is so relevant to our situation.' To my surprise, he handed me a reply to his letter from Frank, one of his sons.

'Maybe you should have asked us why we stopped practising our faith', Frank wrote. 'Yes, you sent us all to Catholic school but really what we were taught did not make sense to us. I had so many questions to ask, but often I was given superficial answers. Maybe the people who taught us didn't believe as strongly as you.

Since growing up I've realised that the world is a small place and that there are many ways to God. Our Church does not have a monopoly on the truth. Maybe religion is just the human race's way of coping with basic insecurity.

I've always objected to the authoritarianism of the Church, objected to the statement that faith is something I must have whether I like it or not.

This is the 1990s. God is insignificant today. Our generation has its own ideas. We don't need God . . .'

As I read Frank's letter I could see how relevant St Paul's words were for David and Kate. It was almost as if God were confirming their own sentiments.

Frank's letter could be anyone's letter – it certainly reflected the feelings of his brothers and sisters.

Maybe when Paul wrote his letter to the Corinthians the situation wasn't too different from today. He was speaking to a world that had many gods. He was speaking to a world that had its own thinking, its own philosophers. The city of Corinth was powerful because of its strategic sea port position. It was a thriving centre for commerce and it was dominated by the temple of Aphrodite, the goddess of love and beauty. In this city, concepts like 'liberty' and 'knowledge' were important. Paul spoke to a very human Church in Corinth, one influenced by all the powers of its day.

What Frank failed to realise, but what is stated clearly in the reading, is that faith is a gift. It is a relationship with God which human beings seek in their heart of hearts. Awareness of this relationship with God can give us the certainty we seek – a strength of certainty which reason alone is unable to confer.

Some say that faith is not taught but caught. Passing it on to others doesn't just mean teaching with authority, but somehow enabling people to catch a glimpse of God in a real situation. It is very difficult to help people catch faith when they live in a society which is opposed to anything which cannot be scientifically proven. But a human being is not just a mind – a thinking machine which can be compartmentalised. We have many dimensions and we communicate and receive in many ways – feeling, intuition, body language and words, for example. Faith is often caught through this sort of indirect communication with others who have faith. Logic obviously has an important part to play because we naturally need to understand what is happening and we want to have things explained. But this reading from Corinthians shows that faith is not just a case of the mind agreeing to something reasonable, particularly in sceptical times. Although faith is sometimes seen as being pushed onto people by Church authority, the Bible talks about a wisdom which is not a human wisdom. It is an openness of mind which allows the God out there to enter into our being.

Many people are not open to this awareness of how God wishes to touch them. They have already rejected religion as irrelevant. They have accepted the idea that we can look to science for explanations of what life is all about; chosen, if you like, to regulate their lives on the basis of the material dimension alone.

Faith may be impossible for them until they learn to develop an open mind, and getting through to them so that their minds may open up may first mean reasoning with them along the lines to which secular thinking may have accustomed them. But faith goes beyond the debating stage and there comes a time when logical reasoning stops and faith begins. It is an initiative of God. If faith were merely a result of our human thinking then all the great academics would enter the realms of faith before those with poorer intellects, and that is not God's way: 'God's weakness is stronger than human strength'.

FOR REFLECTION

1. Is there a right or wrong way to pass on our faith?
2. How can we reveal God's love to someone?
3. How can faith be imparted by living example?

PRAYER

O Lord, save us from anxiety. Let our faith help us commit ourselves to you more fully, to be used as your instruments of peace. Help us to learn to be less concerned about ourselves and more concerned for others. May every new day give us an opportunity to spread your peace for you.

Why My Family?

OUR PLANE BEGAN TO DESCEND towards Kennedy Airport. Another story had ended in my book of experience but somehow we take these encounters with us, tucked away some place for another day. Our flight had been so short, too short, I thought as I bade farewell to David and Kate. They had taught me so much by allowing me to share in a painful real life experience. Somehow we left each other with renewed hope in a God who cares but who doesn't seem to fulfil all our desires.

As I disembarked from the aircraft I realised with pleasure that in a few more days I would be home. I would be able to sleep in my own bed for a few nights, would have time to relax with friends. But I had one more speaking engagement to complete. It was in up-state New York in the city of Buffalo in two days' time, and it had been arranged for me to spend the two intervening days taking in the sights of New York. Although I had never met the family I was going to stay with, I wasn't at all apprehensive – I felt in my bones that I was going to have a good time.

Kennedy Airport is just like any other international airport, with thousands of people milling around. In some ways you could say that airports are like prisons – they hold crowds and never empty. Most of the travellers are too weary to care, and seem to be craving only one thing – rest.

It was late, and I could see the lights of cars coming and going, dropping and picking people up. I wondered if one of these cars was about to provide my escape to a peaceful night's rest. I sat on the balcony awaiting the family's arrival. Below, the streets had a deserted look. Many shops had closed completely, while the others were only trading in the most desultory fashion. Before long, I heard my name being called on the tannoy system. At last to bed, I thought.

Outside the terminal building I met one of the members of the family I was to stay with. He was a middle-aged man; we introduced ourselves and he told me his name was Dan. I noticed immediately that, like me, he seemed completely exhausted.

On the way to his home we said little, apart from the ordinary pleasantries. He told me his wife, Jo, and daughter, Lisa, had already gone to bed, but that I would be able to meet them the next day. As soon as I got to bed I lost consciousness and slept the sleep of total exhaustion.

When I awoke I felt ready to face another day. Pushing aside the door of my bedroom I went out onto the terrace. The garden lay still, soft and damp, the grass grey with dew, every leaf picked out with drops of moisture. Today, I thought, would not be busy: time to relax at last.

After a few minutes, Jo appeared and joined me on the terrace. We started getting to know each other and I found I liked her very much. She was a hospitable, friendly woman and easy to talk to.

When she suggested breakfast I offered to help her prepare it and she accepted. While we were cooking she suddenly excused herself. She was gone for what seemed to be a long time.

Breakfast was ready by the time Jo came back. As we ate, I could hear sounds coming from the room Jo had visited. I had assumed their daughter was at school, but obviously I was wrong. Again, Jo excused herself and disappeared for a while. When she returned she told me her story.

Jo explained that Lisa, their daughter, was retarded. They had not realised this when she was born, but their paediatrician informed Jo of Lisa's condition when she was a few weeks old. It was a terrible shock for them; it had taken Dan a long time to accept it. No parent wants to believe that the child they helped create can be anything less than perfect.

Lisa needed special loving, care and patience. She didn't take her first steps until she was three. When she first came into her parents' room swaying from side to side shouting 'mama and dadda' it was a magnificent achievement which brought tears to their eyes.

Lisa's condition meant that Dan and Jo had to move from a flat to their present home. Shortly after moving Lisa had a febrile convulsion. The doctors told them not to worry too much but it was impossible. She was put on medication to help the fits, but after each one Jo noticed that she was talking less and less and she reverted back to wearing nappies during the day.

One day she sustained severe brain damage. On being told this by the paediatrician Jo found herself shouting, 'It's not fair, but it's just not fair!'

The fits continued until they became quite regular. Lisa no longer spoke and now needed help with feeding. When neighbours and friends became aware of the situation help and sympathy flowed in, but Dan and Jo were becoming exhausted by the pressure of dealing with Lisa. People asked why she could not go into a special home. 'Because she's our child and we love her', Jo protested.

There were many times when they felt hopeless about their lives, wondering what they had done to deserve it. They sometimes cried out to God for help. Dan and Jo decided that they could not expect or demand from Lisa the goals in life that are taken for granted with 'normal' kids. Any achievement, no matter how small, would be celebrated and so when Lisa was able to put on her own coat and socks she was praised and her parents silently rejoiced. Their decision to accept Lisa and her handicap made their lives a little easier. It was very hard work for the parents but life was never routine or dull 'We were even adopted by a stray kitten, I don't know why', laughed Jo.

Not long after Lisa's fourth birthday the fits became even more frequent and different medications were tried for a while. She would get up in the small hours which meant that Dan and Jo were even more exhausted. When it was arranged for Lisa to go into hospital for a few nights to give them a rest they did not enjoy the break because they missed Lisa terribly.

Dan and Jo began to ask God where he was in their lives – couldn't he see their suffering? They always went to Mass on Sundays; they prayed, especially during the low times. Jo told me that God rewarded them in the tremendous support and encouragement that they received from the medics, nurses and many friends and neighbours.

Her handicaps didn't stop Lisa from getting up to mischief. She would come into her parents bedroom and push her wet nappy into Dan's face. One morning they awoke to a loud explosion. On rushing downstairs they found the television had exploded. Lisa stood behind it with an expectant look on her face as if to say, 'At last you got up – now can we have some breakfast?' Her exploits were hilarious but only after the event when her parents' pulses had returned to normal.

One blessing in their lives was the new parish priest, who took a great interest in Lisa. He talked to her rather than through her – so many people are guilty of unintentionally ignoring handicapped people and only talking to their carers. Since his arrival, going to Mass took on a new meaning for Lisa. The priest used to visit regularly and play with Lisa in a way that she could respond to. He even suggested that when she was a little older it would be possible for her to receive Holy Communion.

Although their lives were devoted to Lisa, Dan and Jo still felt guilty. It would make them question whether they were 'doing enough'. Were there areas where they neglected Lisa in their lives? Had they got it right?

Thanks to donations from their church, the whole

family managed a trip to Lourdes. This was a tremendous
healing experience for all of them. Lisa made her first
Holy Communion there, and they partied all day. The
experience of meeting and seeing other handicapped
children – some with worse illnesses than Lisa – helped
Jo and Dan. How could so many people be happy with
such terrible afflictions? This experience brought the
whole family together in a new way. Lisa was not conven-
tionally healed at Lourdes, but a new light shone in her
parents' lives. It was something they could hold onto in
days of darkness.

Today, as Jo sat with me at the breakfast table, it was
one of those days. It was a day when Lisa needed extra
attention. As usual, in a very ordinary way, she was getting it from her mother and would receive it from her
father when he returned from work. What love.

What piece of God's word in the Bible would give
encouragement and hope to this family I thought to
myself . . .

◆━━━◆

*It was before the festival of the Passover, and Jesus knew
that the hour had come for him to pass from this world
to the Father. He had always loved those who were his
in the world, but now he showed how perfect his love
was.*

*They were at supper, and the devil had already put it
into the mind of Judas Iscariot son of Simon to betray
him. Jesus knew that the Father had put everything into
his hands, and that he had come from God and was
returning to God, and he got up from table, removed his
outer garment and, taking a towel, wrapped it round his
waist; he then poured water into a basin and began to
wash the disciples' feet and to wipe them with the towel
he was wearing.*

*He came to Simon Peter who said to him, 'Lord, are
you going to wash my feet?' Jesus answered, 'At the
moment you do not know what I am doing, but later
you will understand'. 'Never!' said Peter 'You shall never*

wash my feet.' Jesus replied, 'If I do not wash you, you can have nothing in common with me'. 'Then, Lord,' said Simon Peter 'not only my feet, but my hands and my head as well!' Jesus said, 'No one who has taken a bath needs washing, he is clean all over. You too are clean, though not all of you are.' He knew who was going to betray him, that was why he said, 'though not all of you are'.

When he had washed their feet and put on his clothes again he went back to the table. 'Do you understand' he said 'what I have done to you? You can call me Master and Lord, and rightly; so I am. If I, then, the Lord and Master, have washed your feet, you should wash each other's feet. I have given you an example so that you may copy what I have done to you.'

(John 13:1–15)

◁═════▷

This was Jesus' last and best gift of love, as he gave the disciples proof of the depth of his affection. Suddenly, he rose from where he was sitting, so suddenly that it didn't occur to the rest to move. He went towards them with a basin of water, rolled up his sleeves in preparation for some manual task. What could this mean? They had seen him do manual work before, but during supper was a very strange time to do it. When he began to wash their feet, the twelve must have been amazed. There must have been times in the past when his behaviour had caused them to wonder and ask questions. Mary of Magdalene had anointed Jesus' feet, but he was a celebrity. They were humbled and ashamed – if they had dared they would have drawn their feet in and protested. Quietly, deliberately, he went down the row and washed their dusty feet, as a slave would do, and then wiped them clean. In his tender way he did it so that they might feel part of him and so that they might understand their future tasks. In the future they would have to do lots of mundane things and would have to treat people with compassion and love.

Only one of them had the courage to protest: Simon, who of late had been called Peter. He was beginning to realise his new status as leader of the twelve. 'Lord, are you going to wash my feet?' he asks. Jesus knew that in Peter, like in us all, there was the good and the not so good, but the essential worth of the individual was the only thing that mattered to him. Jesus had far reaching vision. He could look through the present and beyond it, through weakness and failure and beyond them. He was content to endure, to forgive and to serve. But Peter hadn't travelled that far yet – he drew his feet away and protested.

Jesus knew how to handle Peter. With all his faults there was something between them on which Jesus could invariably rely. Jesus had only to threaten separation and Peter's resistance would vanish. Quietly, therefore, but with the firmness with which he had always treated Peter, he said, 'If I do not wash you, you can have nothing in common with me'. This was enough, in fact it was more than enough. He had touched that tender spot in Peter's heart and in accordance with Peter's personality he rushed from one extreme to the other. Peter loved Jesus, loved him more than he realised. If to be served by Jesus was a condition of their union then he would submit. Let Jesus have all, and more than all, if only in return Peter could be part of him.

Jesus had humbled himself before them; no master in Israel washed feet. But he also wanted to teach them that what he had done was more than an act of humility: it was a sign. Peter had already caught a glimpse of the truth. He had seen that union with Jesus was bound up with being of service to others. 'Do you understand?' Jesus asked them bluntly. He was now asking them to do the same to others. Humility and charity were blended into each other: they were to be each other's servants.

If they were to be his preachers they had to learn to wash the feet of others. If they were to be his witnesses, they had to learn service. If they were to really touch people, their deeds had to accompany their words.

As Jo and I sat sharing breakfast she was getting up to tend to the needs of her daughter, and I saw that her actions were actions of love and self-emptying. Jo and Dan had 'washed the feet' of their daughter for years. I know if I had expressed it to them in these terms they would have denied it. Yet to an outsider it was obvious that these loving parents like many others, were following the example of Jesus. They may not have got it all right all the time. They may not have felt like doing it each time. They may have grumbled periodically. But like Peter, they submitted in the end to the task facing them.

FOR REFLECTION

1. How did Lisa bring out the best in Jo and Dan?
2. How did these parents see Lisa as God's special child to them?
3. How do other parents respond to children with special needs?

PRAYER

Jesus, be my refuge and strength. Help me in times of trouble. Give me the strength to continue so that I can do the little things as well as the big ones for those who need my help. Grant me patience in times of distress and work in me so that I can help those in need.

Why Go On?

MY TWO DAYS IN NEW YORK passed quickly and soon the City of Buffalo was on the horizon: my last conference before flying back to London. It had been a great pleasure staying with Dan, Jo and Lisa and again it was time to move on. Dan drove me to Buffalo, and on the way we were able to reflect and share. I had never seen such countryside outside the pages of a book of fairy tales. The splendour of the scenery somehow helped me to gather my thoughts together for the conference ahead.

When we neared the Conference Centre where I was going to speak, the boulevards had high green trees that the sun was slowly turning chocolate brown. The houses were all different, spaced apart, some big, some small. It was a lovely area. The Conference Centre itself seemed quiet when we finally reached it, its tower giving it an enhanced elegance. This was to be my home for the weekend.

Having said my farewells to Dan, I was shown to my quarters. From my bedroom window I could see the people arriving. There was a cross-section of people, men and women, young and old. This was going to be another opportunity to share the gospel of Jesus with new people, people who would teach me as I endeavoured to teach them.

The conference was in full swing and going very well when one of the participants caught my eye. He was a thoughtful-looking man of middle years, who was confined to a wheelchair. That evening we had a social gathering, and as I went into the bar he and his wife called me over and asked me to join them for a drink. Their names were Mary and Michael.

Despite the masses of people crowding the bar, I felt like we were the only three people in the room. They soon put me at my ease, telling me how much they were enjoying the conference. They had never attended a gathering like this and said they were getting a lot out of it.

Michael soon told me that he suffered from multiple sclerosis, the crippling disease that attacks the central nervous system and which can get progressively worse. In the 1960s he said he had been employed as a salesman in Detroit, but when he was in his late thirties he had felt drawn towards joining the police. 'I was so excited when they accepted me', he said, taking obvious pleasure in the memory.

When he was assigned to street patrol to be 'shown the ropes', he felt he was almost learning to speak again. A police officer has to learn to control his or her words. Everyone's eyes and ears are on you. Every move can be analysed and misinterpreted. In those days, Michael told me, he was only a nominal Christian and went to church only on special occasions.

Shortly after his initial training he moved to rural duties, and during that time he worked on his own. He was kept active and was reasonably fit – the police department forced him to take regular exercise and he learned to keep calm under stress. He shared with me some fascinating stories about his career in the force – it was obvious he had seen life in the raw. Although he was fit, he had been involved in many dangerous incidents and received numerous beatings, many of which were to his head and upper body.

In 1980, he had his first attack of parathesia – a condition which can eventually turn into multiple sclerosis. The condition attacked him every month and would last for about fourteen days, but he was able to return to normal duty after each attack. Michael kept asking himself why he was having these attacks – it felt like a punishment from God.

After six years of it, he fell ill again and this time he was unable to return to work. His specialist told him he had MS. The career he loved was over.

In 1987, Michael retired from the police force on a medical pension. He spent a long time coming to terms with his illness. His life changed radically when he was no longer an active person serving the public. The long days at home on his own while Mary was at work were hard – having nothing to do and no one to speak to made his imagination run riot. And yet, on the whole he said he had managed to find a kind of contentment – he told me he realised that it is not physical strength or dexterity which gives a person dignity, – 'We all have dignity because we are all children of God.'

I was preaching at the Sunday service the next day and I thought it would be good to choose a passage that would speak to Mary and Michael and people like them, a passage that would give them hope.

They came to a small estate called Gethsemane, and Jesus said to his disciples, 'Stay here while I pray'. Then he took Peter and James and John with him. And a sudden fear came over him, and great distress. And he said to them, 'My soul is sorrowful to the point of death. Wait here, and keep awake.' And going on a little further he threw himself on the ground and prayed that, if it were possible, this hour might pass him by. 'Abba (Father)!' he said 'Everything is possible for you. Take this cup away from me. But let it be as you, not I, would have it.' He came back and found them sleeping, and he said to Peter, 'Simon, are you asleep? Had you not the strength to keep awake one hour? You should be awake, and praying not to be put to the test. The spirit is willing, but the flesh is weak.' Again he went away and prayed, saying the same words. And once more he came back and found them sleeping, their eyes were so heavy; and

*they could find no answer for him. He came back a third
time and said to them, 'You can sleep on now and take
your rest. It is all over. The hour has come. Now the Son
of Man is to be betrayed into the hands of sinners.'*

(Mark 14:32–41)

◆━━━━▶

At the gate of the garden, Jesus stood and let the eleven
gather around him. On other occasions they had all gone
into the garden together, but now Jesus asked most of
them to wait for him outside the gate. This time there
was something new in his manner and he seemed to
sense danger. He went inside the gates and beckoned to
only three, Peter, James and John to follow him. On more
than one occasion he had wanted these three to be close
to him, but it had always been to show them something.
These three had seen Jesus transformed in glory in the
past, seen his humanity absorbed in his divinity. Now
his manhood oppressed him with all its weary weight
and he began to grieve, as if he were carrying a burden
that was too much for him. He was terribly sad, as if, at
last, depression and a sense of defeat had overcome his
hitherto never-failing hope and courage. He began to be
afraid, although he had never shown any fear before. He
had walked unscathed through every trap and every
threatening crowd – now he seemed to be at a loss, as if
he did not know which way to turn. In his distress, he
feared being left alone, although in the past he had gone
to the desert and the mountains to speak with his Father.
He looked at the three as if he depended on them. He
implored them to stay with him and keep awake.

Peter, James and John must have looked at Jesus in
amazement. He was no longer the strong man, the auth-
oritative figure who had everything under control. He
staggered forward through the darkness and fell on the
ground. He was unable to even support himself. He
shouted in agony and distress. He prayed a prayer that
was unlike any other he had made. He wanted the pain
to pass. He wanted to be rescued by his Father. Whatever

had happened in the past no one could break the union which existed between himself and the Father, but it was as if he wished to break that bond now. As he lay on the ground he knew what lay before him. There was no one's shame and confusion, no one's remorse and desperation, no one's agony of sorrow and repentance that Jesus did not share in this time in the garden. It was an agony whose mystery we cannot hope to fathom. But we can understand enough to appreciate the pain which could drag forth the cry, 'Father take this away from me'.

This was the cry of God suffering, the cry of a broken man. yet it was also the cry of a man of infinite strength. He prayed against himself when he cried, 'but let it be as you not I would have it'. This prayer made real all that he had ever prayed: he had told everyone in the past that he had come to do the Father's will not his own.

But if the Father allowed his only son to suffer so much, surely Jesus' friends should have given him some comfort? How many promises had they given him that they would never desert him? For an hour or more he lay on the ground, crushed beneath a burden that was too much for him, and all he wanted was that little bit of support. But he came back to them and found them asleep.

The hour had been long. Their minds had wandered. They had just come from supper and would have had a few glasses of wine. The silence had made them drowsy. A few minutes before they had been so valiant and fervent in their own strength. Jesus felt it; how could he but feel it? He was disappointed. Nowhere do we see Jesus as more manifestly human than when he responds to a show of friendship or rejection. But he did not complain; he was not resentful. He admonished Peter not out of malice but because much would depend on Peter. The future itself depended on him in fact. The three disciples in their sleepiness stopped noticing the condition of Jesus. They might have pulled themselves together for a little while yet weariness came upon them again and they yielded to sleep once more. Jesus struggled alone.

As I preached my sermon I could see that Michael was identifying with it. He too had wished on occasion that things be different. He too, like Jesus, experienced the pain of being completely alone in his sufferings. He, too, knew what it was like to have other people not understand and be able to provide no comfort. He, too, prayed: 'Father take this from me'. Yet we all know that whatever any of us suffers, or can suffer, Jesus himself suffered as no other. Sharing in his suffering allows us to enter the door of pain and be comforted.

FOR REFLECTION

1. What are my greatest fears in life?
2. How do I cope with pain, especially when I am alone?
3. In what way is Jesus' suffering helpful to me?

PRAYER

Lord Jesus Christ teach us to walk more trustfully in your ways. Help us in times of doubt and loneliness to see ourselves as you saw yourself. Sustain us in times of great pain. Give generously to us when we feel low and never abandon us to our weaknesses.

Why My Relationship?

MY TIME IN THE UNITED STATES had come to an end. I was excited to think that soon I would be home again, but there was also a degree of sadness. I had met so many lovely people in America and made lots of friends. It is a strange paradox in our lives that we can feel joy and sorrow at the same time. Michael and Mary insisted that they drive me to the airport.

Once I was safely on the plane, I realised it would be quite late when we landed at Heathrow. It was going to be difficult for me to get home to Birmingham. I decided to call Ann, an old friend who lived near the airport to see if she would pick me up.

Ann had a very unhappy childhood. She never felt loved or wanted and as a result she grew up desperate for some-one to love her. She married the first man she went out with.

The first years of the marriage were happy ones. She had her husband, her family and her home. She had never really felt fulfilled sexually, but she tried to ignore it. Since her husband was the only man she had ever been to bed with she had no way of making comparisons and thought that every woman felt like she did.

While the children were very young she felt needed, but once they had grown up she became emotionally insecure again. She noticed that her husband treated her badly, as if she were just another possession he owned. He worked to pay the bills and felt that this alone was an adequate contribution to the relationship. He went out on his own a lot and they rarely communicated on a level which satisfied Ann emotionally. Steadily she lost her confidence and became convinced that she was inadequate as a person. She felt she lived in a loveless marriage, that she was just a housekeeper her husband went to bed with. She didn't feel that they ever made love, just had sex, and she felt bitter and frustrated. It was inevitable she would respond if someone else came into her life.

From the day it happened, she loved him. Although she thought about him constantly she had no intentions of having an affair, but this kind of situation never stands still and it happened despite her intentions. This man came first in Ann's life, before God, before her husband and children. When she felt guilty before God she would tell herself he would understand and forgive her. When she thought about her husband she would tell herself that he deserved it. When she thought of cheating on her children she would justify it by saying that what they didn't know would do them no harm. It seemed her love affair was everything that she had ever dreamed of, and she cheated and lied to justify herself.

But it was destined to go wrong. She loved him unconditionally but she found out that there were other women. He wanted Ann totally, but then he would break off the relationship for weeks at a time. The strain of trying to behave normally at home nearly forced Ann to have a nervous breakdown, and it was inevitable that her husband and children would notice that there was something amiss. Ann, however, was blind to everything except her own feelings. She constantly lied to get herself out of awkward situations; suspicion is one thing, but she ensured that she was never actually caught.

She would manage to get away to visit imaginary friends. She gave wrong telephone numbers and asked others to cover up for her while she would spend weekends with her lover. He was a wealthy businessman so he had access to hotels on business trips. He was married too and his marriage was also an unhappy one. He, too, was insecure – they needed each other.

But gradually the relationship became a battleground. He turned out to be very much like her husband; he would not discuss anything except superficially. When it suited him he would turn up asking forgiveness and expect Ann to behave as if nothing had happened. He wanted to keep all his options open and for a long time his need for Ann kept her going. At these times she was deliriously happy, but of course it was always short-lived. She needed security in the relationship, but that was the one thing he could never give her. He would not make a decision to marry her or leave his wife. Nor would he end the relationship. She would beg him to decide what he wanted, but he wouldn't.

Ann became aware of all the hurt that she was causing her husband and family, and of the almost constant pain she was in. She tried desperately to explain to her lover that they had to leave their respective homes and make a new life together, but he wasn't prepared to do it. He was aware of his business reputation; leaving his wife for another woman could prove disastrous both financially and socially. He said he loved Ann but was not prepared to commit himself to her.

She realised she was the one who had to be strong. After much soul-searching she knew that she had to have the courage to end it.

◆━━━◆

If I have all the eloquence of men or of angels, but speak without love, I am simply a gong booming or a cymbal clashing. If I have the gift of prophecy, understanding all the mysteries there are, and knowing everything, and if I have faith in all its fulness, to move mountains, but without love, then I am nothing at all. If I give away all that I possess, piece by piece, and if I even let them take my body to burn it, but am without love, it will do me no good whatever.

Love is always patient and kind; love is never boastful or conceited; it is never rude or selfish; it does not take offence, and is not resentful. Love takes no pleasure in other people's sins but delights in the truth; it is always ready to excuse, to trust; to hope, and to endure whatever comes.

Love does not come to an end. But if there are gifts of prophecy, the time will come when they must fail; or the gift of languages, it will not continue for ever; and knowledge – for this, too, the time will come when it must fail. For our knowledge is imperfect and our prophesying is imperfect; but once perfection comes, all imperfect things will disappear. When I was a child, I used to talk like a child, and think like a child, and argue like a child, but now I am a man, all childish ways are put behind me. Now we are seeing a dim reflection in a mirror; but then we shall be seeing face to face. The knowledge that I have now is imperfect; but then I shall know as fully as I am known.

In short, there are three thing that last: faith, hope and love; and the greatest of these is love.

(1 Corinthians 13:1–13)

◄────►

Throughout Ann's affair she never lost her faith in God. She continued to go to church. She constantly begged God's understanding and forgiveness, and she really wanted God to be on her side. Before her affair she was dreadfully unhappy, completely unfulfilled in most areas of her life. She had prayed that God would bring love into her life, and she thought her prayer had been answered when she met this other man. We are often told to be careful what we pray for – we just might get it. On thinking back she didn't really know what she had been asking for, but what she got was never worth all the misery it produced.

She always loved this part of St Paul's letter to the Corinthians. During her affair she would try and interpret it in many different ways. She knew that the love that she was indulging herself in was wrong, but she would tell herself that it was beautiful and joyous. She would tell herself that it had to be from God.

She would spend time on her own in church reasoning with God, begging him to understand and asking forgiveness for her weaknesses while at the same time telling him that she couldn't help it, couldn't stop it. She would tell him that he made her and he must understand. Were these useless selfish prayers? To make up for what she was doing she tried very hard to love people. She worked for charity and ran herself ragged trying to help people who needed her. She was trying to bargain with God, trading Christian acts of love for illicit love. Deep down, she knew very well what St Paul really meant. He spoke of pure unselfish love not sinful secret love, that causes pain.

'Now we are seeing a dim reflection in a mirror; but then we shall be seeing face to face. The knowledge that I have now is imperfect: but then I shall know as fully as I am known.' Ann would read these words and plead ignorance. She didn't know why she felt like she did or behaved like she did. When all was revealed she would understand, but until then she would put her imperfections behind her for a little longer. She wanted passionate physical love. She wanted to live her life for this man. What she didn't realise was that this sort of love can cool. It cannot last. All relationships change: in a true relationship in God, love will deepen, respect will grow and true companionship materialise. How can this happen within an affair?

An affair always has to be secret. Feelings cannot be acknowledged openly – they are hidden away by lying and cheating, which given time, will sour the relationship. Ann clung to what she thought she wanted, and tried to convince herself that St Paul's writing was encouraging her to hold onto the 'real thing'.

Her husband went through hell. He thought her lover would take her away for good. He worried every time she went out in case she was meeting him, as he suffered the intense pain of rejection. But Ann eventually realised that even despite it all her husband still loved her and did not want to lose her. When she announced it was all over he forgave her and welcomed her back into their marriage.

It turned out that Ann's husband's love for her *was* that of St Paul: patient, forgiving, accepting. He was not able to meet all her needs but he did offer her faithfulness and loyalty, things her lover didn't know the meaning of. He is still not sensitive to all Ann's feelings but he is a hard-working and honest man and he is always trying. When she looks at him now perhaps the 'dim reflection in the mirror' is not so dark. Because of where she has been she understands him better and appreciates his good points that much more. As her earthly understanding has increased, she realises how much more deep will be our heavenly understanding. Since her affair she understands more clearly how totally forgiving God is.

Ann suffered badly after the affair ended: the pain of parting, the guilt of hurting so many people. She was helped in coming to terms with it all by the real love of her family. Trying to find love had brought misery, but God permits us to learn from pain like this.

It all could have been different. Her marriage could have folded and she could have lost everything. Instead she has found the knowledge that true love has a permanence that permeates everything.

FOR REFLECTION

1. What is your understanding of love in relationships?
2. How do you cope when love goes wrong?
3. Does God show us a right and wrong way to love?

PRAYER

Lord Jesus Christ you came to teach us how to love. Show us always the need to turn our relationships over to you. Grant that in our loving we have the humility to give and receive forgiveness. Always walk with us even when we have got it wrong. Show us the right way and help us to see clearly the meaning of true love.

Why This Illness?

ON ARRIVAL AT HEATHROW I called Ann and her husband and they came to pick me up. It was good to see them again. In spite of the traumas that they have gone through they are managing to rebuild their relationship, and they are determined to make their marriage work.

It was good to get home. It seemed such a long time since I had left but everything looked so familiar. My desk seemed showered from heaven with letters and it was raining outside. Winter was approaching.

Despite all the mail that surrounded me I knew that I had to prepare a sermon for Sunday. It was to be on the healing power of love. As I worked, I heard the laughter of a child walking with its parents outside my window. I looked out and on seeing the family they reminded me of another family I had been very close to when I was a young newly-ordained priest.

Paul and Joyce were a couple in their early thirties and had one child, Joanne, who was at primary school. Paul was a self-employed plumber; Joyce a shop assistant. They were a friendly down-to-earth couple and were actively involved in the life of their parish. Paul co-ordinated the transport for church on Sundays; Joyce gave of her time, her love and her energy in any way she could. She was always the first to volunteer if help was needed, and made cakes, jams, soft toys and children's clothes for the parish get-togethers and fairs.

Occasionally on an evening off I would go to visit them. During these times they would share their desire for a deeper faith, a more meaningful prayer life, but they felt they had little time to do this. They were always so busy. One evening when I went around to see them, I noticed they both seemed preoccupied and unable to concentrate on the conversation. I asked if anything was troubling them. Joyce said at last that she had been to see the doctor about a lump in her breast. She had to go into hospital a week later for investigations. There was a chance it could be malignant. My heart sank as I struggled for some reassuring words. Joyce saw my confusion and perked up. 'Oh, I'll be all right', she said, 'it's just a check up.' Then she changed the topic of conversation.

A week later I visited Joyce in hospital. As soon as I walked into the ward I knew all was not well. Paul sat holding Joyce's hand and Joanne was sitting on the bed cuddling up to her mother. Joyce looked flushed and she had clearly been crying. Seeing me walking towards her she tried to smile but couldn't. I spent some time with them, just listening. They told me Joyce had had to have a mastectomy and would be needing further treatment. They were very upset and fearful.

Before I left I laid my hands on Joyce and prayed over her. I ended with the Our Father, but I noticed that Paul didn't join in. He looked me straight in the eyes and said that he was angry. How had this loving God allowed this to happen to his wife? She hadn't done anything wrong – she was a good person. I hesitated for a moment and confessed to him that I couldn't answer his question. All I knew was that she was receiving proper treatment from professional medical staff and that she was surrounded by a loving family. I tried to assure him that it was important to persevere with prayers for her recovery.

Joyce remained in hospital for a while. Initially she was quite low, anxious about her treatment and fearful about the future. Paul was worried too. He had found it a humbling experience to see Joanne trusting in God while he had his doubts.

The family's lifestyle changed as Joyce had to give up work. Because Paul was self-employed, he lost a lot of money taking time off to be with Joyce during her chemo-therapy. Financially it was a struggle for them, but one thing the illness taught them was how unimportant money really is when the worst comes.

During the first few weeks of her treatment Joyce was easily tired, and restricted in what she could do. As a naturally active person she found it very difficult to stay still. She was frustrated that her body could not respond to what her mind was telling it. She slowly realised that she had to allow others to show their care and love by doing for her all the things that she used to do for others. But it was difficult.

As she began to recuperate Joyce did a lot of thinking. Things that she had taken for granted before she now appreciated. She sat in the garden, watched the birds, saw the trees and the flowers in a new light. Her conval-escence gave her a new appreciation of creation and, in particular, the gift of life.

The family also came together in a new way. Their love for each other grew as they pulled together. Speaking with the family just eight months after Joyce's operation, they all said how they had changed, how Joyce's illness had helped them get their priorities right.

Although they had doubts and fears, somehow God had used the situation. Where there is love, there is God.

❖═══❖

In the evening of that same day, the first day of the week, the doors were closed in the room, where the disciples were, for fear of the Jews. Jesus came and stood among them. He said to them, 'Peace be with you', and he showed them his hands and his side. The disciples were filled with joy when they saw the Lord, and he said to them again, 'Peace be with you . . . '

(John 20:19–21)

❖═══❖

No one can fully understand or appreciate what the disciples were experiencing on that first day of the week. Jesus had been crucified three days before. He had left them alone. We would have to be there to truly understand the trauma they were experiencing, but, in a strange way, we have all been there. Paul, Joyce and Joanna certainly have been. The disciples were experiencing fear. For the disciples it was fear of the Jews, for Joyce it was fear of cancer; the circumstances were different but the end product was the same: Joyce and her family are representative of the many people who have to come to terms with the fear that serious illness brings about.

Fear for the disciples of what the Jews would do to them; fear for Joyce of what her illness would do to her and to her family. Two thousand years span these events and yet the emotion is the very same. What did fear cause the disciples to do? They closed the doors of the house; they might even have bolted them and put heavy objects against them. Their master and mentor had gone. Joyce's health had gone, taken by a life-threatening illness. Paul's anger at this happening to his wife caused him to close himself up to the possibility of God being behind it. He was afraid and his fear turned to an isolating anger.

Joyce's initial reaction was fear. But soon her God-given cheerfulness seemed to prevail; although she was afraid she allowed her fear to be overcome by letting Jesus get a foothold in her doorway. Her ability to be open to prayer gave Jesus the space to bring her peace. What Jesus gives is not, first of all, a feeling of peace. The peace of Christ is an invisible, graced state of life. We could compare it to a state of health. We may or may not feel our health – it is simply a condition of an organism granted to us by nature. So it is with the state of peace granted us by the Lord. A feeling of good health, of vital well-being, may flow from our healthy condition, yet it may be imperceptible, even absent at times. The reverse is also true – a person may feel in excellent shape yet may not be healthy any longer. A deadly disease may be eating away inside.

The same is true of the state of peace. It is the condition of reconciliation with God. The word 'peace' in John's gospel is like the word 'truth', 'light' and 'joy'. They all express facets of the gift of life that Jesus has brought from the Father. Joyce saw that gift properly when she became aware of the beauty of nature all around her. She had been oblivious to it before. The gift of life implies a basic state of peace with God, and we can be in that state, yet not be free from discord or agitation. The peace that Jesus gives means far more than a sense of safety and composure in the face of danger: it speaks of the deepest relationship between ourselves and our God.

Joanne's prayer was answered: it brought hope. Joyce felt uplifted which influenced Paul. Notice how God uses people, and works through them. Negative words can bring us down; positive words can encourage. When we open ourselves to the possibilities it can be incredibly powerful. So often we limit God, but the pull of our fear is never stronger than the Peace of Christ. Jesus came and stood with Paul, Joyce and Joanne in their suffering. He came to bring peace, not necessarily to take the problem away. Jesus is both crucified and risen. Scripture says, 'He showed them his hands and his side' – the scars of suffering were still evident on his body. He speaks of 'peace' still showing the marks of crucifixion. He made the disciples focus on him, not on the Jews, the object of their fear. His peace washed away fear. Joyce, too, was still showing the physical scars of her illness and she worried about future complications. But she was at peace.

When the disciples recognised Jesus they were 'filled with joy'. Not only did he bring peace but his very presence was a source of joy. Paul and Joyce's lifestyle changed. They had to give up their jobs for a while, but they realised money wasn't a priority for them. The joy of the deepening of their love was more important. Family life gave new joy to their being – Joyce had become the wounded healer.

Sometimes we allow our experience of peace to spread itself in our daily lives, but we do not always accept it as a gift. We set our hearts on too many other things. We struggle to achieve peace; we do not see it as a gift. We are driven by the futile hope that peace will be ours when our dreams and desires come true, but this is the shallow, transitory peace of the world. The reception of God's peace brings about the greatest miracle of all: internal peace and acceptance.

FOR REFLECTION

1. Where are the areas of fear in your own life?
2. How can you allow the peace of Jesus into your pain and suffering?
3. What are the priorities in your life? Why?

PRAYER

Lord Jesus, grant us your peace. Grant that we may be free from fear. Give us your peace, a peace of union with you, and contentment within ourselves. Make us less eager for incidental gratifications and let our desire for peace surpass all other desires. Give us also the ability to cast out fear from others.

Why This Addiction?

─────

I WAS BACK IN HARNESS again. My Sunday sermon went well, and now I was off to the north east of England where I had been asked to give a retreat to a group of men just outside Newcastle. I decided to take the night train so that I could read and relax for a while.

I got myself comfortable in my carriage, which initially was littered with suitcases. As the journey progressed, the train gradually emptied as passengers got off. Within a few hours, only myself and one other man sitting opposite me remained. While the compartment was full he had seemed unfriendly and withdrawn, but now he looked more relaxed. He was tall, dark and looked to be in his forties. He was smartly dressed, but his eyes seemed weary beyond his years. Before long, he seemed to want to talk, and I was happy to respond. He told me his name was James and that he was an alcoholic.

At the first meeting of Alcoholics Anonymous he attended, James was told he was beginning a process of liberation. Everyone was welcoming and friendly, and spoke honestly and freely about the horrors of their alcoholism. Several of them spoke about a 'higher power' which had saved them and enabled them to lead a normal life. James was asked to share his story, and he told me how he had admitted to being an alcoholic at that meeting, but not out of conviction, rather as an attempt to remain inconspicuous. Deep down he resented the others. He resented what he regarded as their naivety.

How could he go about saying things like 'One day at

a time', or 'Let go, let God'? How could these empty phrases relieve the misery of the dull ache that was his life? He had become incapable of rational thought and could not begin to articulate his real feelings. As a child he had always had a feeling of loneliness and inadequacy. Now, listening to the people at that meeting, he felt nothing but despair. They spoke of broken marriages, lost jobs and financial ruin. How could he speak of the mental anguish, dark depression and crippling fear that rendered simple tasks impossible? No one would understand. And so James's drinking continued.

It was alcohol that helped him socialise and freed him from the shackles of self-consciousness, as the magic liquid brought temporary peace and serenity. Now he was told that this same elixir of life was making his fears and depression worse. Doctors had warned him but he couldn't believe it. Nothing seemed to get through to him not even the warning that he would soon die if he continued drinking. He was unable or unwilling to see any danger. Lies and deception were the order of the day, and in fact, he was now unable to distinguish between fact and fantasy. He would get up in the morning to a drinking session which could last all day. He was a lorry driver and he sometimes thought that one good tug of the wheel would end it all. As the addiction tightened its grip, James would drink until he blacked out almost every day. On one such occasion his wife found him in a pool of blood which necessitated hospital treatment. People thought that while he was there he would see sense but all he could think of was getting out and into the nearest pub. His wife and family were suffering terribly but James was unable to stop.

Eventually he agreed to enter a hospital that specialised in the treatment of alcoholism. In hospital, propped up in bed and suitably drugged, things were fine. But he couldn't stay on this type of medication for ever. When the doctor started to wean him off it, James began to experience the pain of reality again. He threatened to leave. The doctor replied, 'You are the alcoholic – it's your life. You can't run away from yourself, and if you don't stop trying you'll soon be dead.' James suddenly realised that he was useless – to himself, his family and everyone else. If he ran away it would only mean that at some future date he would be back in hospital in the same state – that is if he were still alive.

This was the beginning of his understanding that something was seriously wrong in his life and needed urgent attention. James said that the doctor's words were delivered in such a matter-of-fact way that it brought him to a sudden halt. It *was* his life. It *was* his problem and no one else's. He had become used to blaming others but he suddenly saw the truth and realised it was no use doing this anymore. His life had been one of constantly running from reality, never being able to face it.

He told me he was like Chuang-tzu in the ancient Chinese saga. Chuang-tzu was afraid of his own shadow, which followed him everywhere. He decided to run away from it, but it kept pace with him effortlessly. Seeing this, he ran faster and faster, until he dropped dead from exhaustion. He should have sat down in the shade and then it would have disappeared. James was like that. The 'black dog' within, which he feared so much, was always with him – he would never shake it off by running away.

The effect of James' drinking on his family had been devastating. When he realised what he had done to them he was hit by enormous guilt and depression. The dark journey towards sanity and sobriety was a difficult one as he faced his fears and confronted his weaknesses. It took a long time, but now at least he is able to face life without alcohol. He told me that he had to face the pain of being human to know the joy of being human. Life, by its nature, is pain and joy mixed together. James is still a recovering alcoholic who has to accept that he is not everything he would like to be. Years ago, at that meeting, he had scorned the slogan, 'One day at a time'. Now it is a way of life.

*While he was still speaking, Judas one of the twelve
came up with a number of men armed with swords and
clubs, sent by the chief priests and the scribes and the
elders. Now the traitor had arranged a signal with them.
'The one I kiss' he had said 'He is the man. Take him
in charge and see he is well guarded when you lead him
away.'*

(Mark 14:43–4)

Jesus gave himself up to his enemies of his own accord.
He had given Judas the chance to avoid his crime, but by
this time Judas was not to be won. His heart had long
since hardened; he had thrown in his lot with the priests
and elders. When he would later claim his reward of
thirty pieces of silver no one could say that he didn't
deserve it. Jesus and Judas had parted friends earlier on
and they met as friends again that same night. They
kissed. Now was the moment for Judas to fulfil his con-
tract. Jesus stood there alone, the lights of their lanterns
picking him out in the darkness. He would still have
saved Judas if Judas had chosen to be saved, but he would
not compel him. Judas had a choice.

Jesus had never compelled anyone to do anything, nor
would he ever do so. Judas was allowed to do his worst.
Jesus could warn Judas, as many people had warned
James on the ramifications of his drinking sprees. Jesus
could keep Judas close to him; he could trust him; he could
give him special advice; he could wash his feet. He
could call him a friend and not a servant, give him the
power of miracles, send him out to preach in his name.
Judas had shared all the honour of the other eleven apos-
tles. But Jesus could do no more: *it was Judas' life*. James'
doctor and those who cared about him could admonish,
warn, help, support and encourage, but they could not
change the 'inner' man.

Jesus did not condemn Judas for his actions: condem-
nation belonged to the Father. Judas was his own. He had
chosen him. Whatever Judas did Jesus would not abandon

the friendship, and would even make an appeal to him at the eleventh hour. He spoke to Judas, while the hands of betrayal were still on him, and all of nature seemed to cry out against the shameful deed that was being done. Luke tells us Jesus whispered to Judas the last words Judas would ever hear from his lips. 'Judas', he asked, 'are you betraying the Son of Man with a kiss?' (Luke 22:48).

It was a terrible indictment: there was not a word too many nor a word too few. Jesus was the master of language and nowhere is it more evident than in this concise statement. James' doctor had been just as blunt when he told him that he would die if he did not change his life.

James told me that he identified with Judas in the Bible. He felt that by his abuse of alcohol he had thrown away the love others had for him. He said he had betrayed himself, his family and everyone else who cared about him, and indeed we could say that he had. But the difference between James and Judas was that James ultimately chose to save himself. When Jesus asked Judas what he was doing, his words had no effect because Judas had put himself beyond Jesus' reach. James, however, allowed the doctor's words to alter the course of his life. Unlike Judas, James seized the chance to save himself.

Following his decision to turn his life around, we can see that James' resemblance to Judas ended, and he became instead like Jesus in this same piece of Scripture. Jesus did not try to escape arrest; likewise James stopped trying to escape reality. Although they had horrors awaiting them, both bravely stood their ground and confronted the situation head on.

James had been like Judas, throwing away the gift of life, but he finally chose to save that gift. He was willing to assent to the higher power which enabled him to live 'one day at a time'.

FOR REFLECTION

1. Do you really believe that God can bring us to a point where he can speak to us? How?
2. Has God allowed you the freedom to reach 'rock bottom'? When? How did you respond?
3. How do you cope when you feel that you have betrayed others?

PRAYER

I ask you, Jesus, to walk with me through my darkest hours. When I feel that there is no way out of my situation, then teach me to live one moment at a time. Never let me lose hope, even in the blackest moment. Help me always to face the reality of my situation, despite the pain, and allow me to grow as a result.

Why This Uselessness?

JAMES' STORY ENABLED ME to help some of the men on the retreat. His story, which he gave me permission to share, stimulated much conversation and helped some of them to open up their own lives. When the retreat was over I had to travel to a preaching engagement in Scotland, so I headed back to the station to catch a train to Edinburgh.

The atmosphere in my compartment was stuffy but pleasant. It was mostly full of young people on their way back to university in Edinburgh. One young man was recounting his recent trip to Florence and he kept us entertained until we finally arrived at Waverley Station.

The atmosphere was still dull and humid as I stopped off the train. I had to wait a while for my connection to Glasgow, so I decided to escape to one of the city's small pubs. This would kill some time and enable me to quench my thirst. I found a quiet little pub at the back of the train station – few people were about at that time of day. I noticed one man speaking loudly to the bar attendant. He was obviously unhappy about something. It didn't take him too long to spot me, and I knew that I too, willing or unwilling, was going to hear his story . . .

Alf had started work at fifteen with a big manufacturing company He thought he had done well for himself because this company did not take 'just anyone', but usually employed only people with good exam results. When Alf had been employed by this company he never thought about looking for another job again. He started on the assembly lines and after a couple of years progressed to checker, then supervisor. Because he was progressing so well he decided that his promotional prospects would be even better if he were better qualified academically. So, at night-school, he took proper exams and, at only 25, he became the manager of the Parts Division.

At night-school he had met Jane. They got on so well that, about the same time as his promotion, they got married. They had great things going for them. They had a mortgage, a good car and a wide circle of friends. They decided to start a family and were fortunate enough to have three healthy sons. Jane gave up work to care for the children but they were still comfortable on Alf's salary. And, after twenty years of working and ten years of marriage, things seemed perfect. In fact they were improving all the time. Alf and Jane bought a bigger car and moved to a nicer area where the property was much more expensive. They had achieved a comfortable lifestyle.

The recession started quietly and whilst Alf felt vaguely concerned, he wasn't terribly worried. His company's business was booming; why should he worry? Even as the recession had taken hold of his company's competitors, forcing them to close down, Alf was unaware that his position was threatened. But, like a thief in the night, hard times crept up on Alf's company. The management decided that some pruning of the workforce had to take place. Long consultations followed but Alf still didn't get over-concerned. He thought he was in an excellent position. After all, he was youngish, talented and, as he thought, indispensable. The first redundancies were announced and Alf was not among them. There was sadness among those who were left, but after a month the company had readjusted to a smaller workforce and all seemed well.

The next wave of redundancies came as a shock because this time they included managerial staff as well as shop-floor workers. To his horror, Alf found his name was on this list. The realisation of what it meant only sank in when he left the building for the last time. Now what was he going to do? He had never been out of work before.

When his redundancy pay ran out, Alf faced the stark reality of unemployment. He signed on for unemployment benefit. He began to look desperately for work. It should have been easy for him; he was well-qualified. But despite all his efforts nothing materialised.

Joining the queues looking for work was a humiliating experience. It seemed as if all the benefit office staff were sixteen and wet behind the ears but he tried to ignore that. He started to write letters and complete application forms and then waited. Few of these letters were even acknowledged. Those who did reply usually just said the post had been filled. Some companies did say that he was under-qualified – while others said he was over-qualified. He had one or two interviews, but the jobs went to younger people who had just left University. At one of the interviews Alf was told, bluntly, that he was too old. This thoroughly deflated him. How could he be too old at thirty-five?

Before Alf knew where he was, he had been out of work for six months. The strain was beginning to show on him and his family. The hopelessness of the situation was putting terrible strain on Alf and Jane's relationship. Spending so much time together made them irritable with each other. Alf told me that it was easier for him to stay in the pub than be at home and get all the 'hassle'.

As the months became a year, the mortgage payments were behind, but Alf had reached the stage where he didn't really care anymore. His pride, his dignity, his self-respect had gone. No one was interested in him. He felt he didn't exist. Even the unemployment office didn't call him by his name. 'You're one of the LTU [long-term unemployed], are you?', one of the staff asked loudly one day. It sounded like a disease.

When I met Alf his family had lost their home and were living in council property. They were in a state of

complete despair. Alf's final comment to me was, 'How
can anyone know how degrading it is to be unemployed?'

◆━━━━▶

*We are only the earthenware jars that hold this treasure,
to make it clear that such an overwhelming power comes
from God and not from us. We are in difficulties on
all sides, but never cornered; we see no answer to our
problems, but never despair; we have been persecuted,
but never deserted; knocked down, but never killed;
always, wherever we may be, we carry with us in our
body the death of Jesus, so that the life of Jesus, too,
may always be seen in our body. Indeed, while we are
still alive, we are consigned to our death every day, for
the sake of Jesus, so that in our mortal flesh the life of
Jesus, too, may be openly shown . . .*

*Yes, the troubles which are soon over, though they
weigh little, train us for the carrying of a weight of eternal glory which is out of all proportion to them. And so
we have no eyes for things that are visible, but only for
things that are invisible; for visible things last only for
a time, and the invisible things are eternal.*

(2 Corinthians 4:7–12; 16–18)

◆━━━━▶

Fundamentally, Alf felt that as one of 'the unemployed'
he was no longer a real person. But does having work
give a person dignity? Doesn't every man and woman
have an innate dignity, regardless of what they do for a
living? St Paul's words make it clear that a person has
dignity because God gives it to each person in their own
right. Work may be important, but a person has value
even without a job, because people have supreme value
in their very essence and being. This is the first and most
fundamental thing I would have liked Alf to realise. This
reading suggests that each person is a creation of infinite
worth.

Jesus met men and women in ordinary situations in
their everyday lives, and by his attitude to them and his

activities among them he demonstrated his understanding of personhood. He saw beyond the externals of life, the distinctions of class, the disparities of living conditions and the shame of corruption, to the priceless value of human life itself. Jesus saw the real people and valued every one of them equally.

Sometimes, as in Alf's case, the individual gets lost in the crowd. Many companies don't seem to care about the real person – they are only interested in getting the job done. For Jesus, the person is the opposite of a machine, is not merely a bearer of borrowed values.

In a series of comparisons, Jesus expressed his belief that people are creatures of the highest value. He contrasted the person with the most cherished institution of the day – there was no custom so firmly established and fiercely defended in Jesus' day as that of keeping the Sabbath. Jesus sought to shake people free from the shackles of custom and teach them that no job or institution has greater worth than the human life for which it was instituted: 'The sabbath was made for man', he said, 'not man for the sabbath' (Mark 2:27).

Jesus declares that people's value exceeds that of all the created universe. 'And indeed what can a man offer in exchange for his life', he asks (Mark 8:37). To lose one's true selfhood is to lose what nothing can buy back. The money that Alf earned to purchase his bigger house and his more up-to-date car did not give him extra dignity. The whole material universe is nothing compared with the intrinsic importance of life itself.

The teaching and actions of Jesus exhibited a regard for people which was more than a mere kindly fellow-feeling, for Jesus was not just a good-natured humanist. His thinking was based on a recognition of the kinship between ourselves and God. Because God became man, he has given historic essence to human dignity. Because Jesus became man, he confronts us where we are in time and space. He is able to ask us who we think we are. He is able to question our priorities and sanctify even our unemployment. In the eyes of the world, dignity is won or earned, yet in the eyes of God it is given as a gift: 'We are only the earthenware jars that hold the treasure'.

The dignity of human beings is also shown perfectly in the story of the Prodigal Son (Luke 15:11–32). In this story, after the son has been unemployed, his father awaits his return with joy and expectation. Such is the value that Jesus puts upon this person, that he says the prodigal's father's heart is stirred to its depths.

Alf felt that in the age of technology he could be replaced by a machine. The size and power of the company he had helped to build eventually devoured him, and the competition to own bigger and better things had squashed his self-worth. Alf became a self-estranged person, an alien in his own world.

St Paul's words reassure us that our significance, self-worth and dignity are a God-given right. Scripture shows us that we matter because we are precious to God, and we are all equal in his love.

FOR REFLECTION

1. Do you consider your identity and self-worth to come from God, or from what you do for a living?
2. Is it within your power to decide your own future? Why?
3. Do you feel accepted as a person by God? By others? In what ways?

PRAYER

Lord Jesus, help me to accept myself as I am. Look upon me and show me my dignity as a person. I know that often my destiny is in the hands of others; guide their dealings with me so that they respect me as a human being. Never let me lose hope, even when I feel isolated and powerless.

Why These Divisions?

MY TRAIN PULLED INTO Glasgow Central. Glasgow is a city like any other major European metropolis. But for me it was like coming home, as it is the city where my mother and father married and lived.

Glasgow is the home of two 'factions': Catholic and Protestant. The influx of people from Ireland has created a large Catholic community in the predominantly Protestant city, and even in sport, for example, there are divisions along denominational lines, with Celtic traditionally being the 'Catholic team', Rangers the 'Protestant team'.

Naturally, the division causes real problems for people, and there can be difficulties when two people of different denominations get married. The clash between the denominations was very real to John and Clare, a young Glasgow couple I knew.

John was a civil engineer, Clare, an infant teacher. Their own children, Matthew and Rachel, were seven and five respectively and both attended the local Catholic school. The words 'Catholic' and 'Protestant' even the wider term 'Christian', were sensitive ones for this couple. After eight years of marriage, Christianity was a subject on which they had agreed to differ.

Although they married in Clare's Catholic Church, their wedding day was the last time that John had set foot inside a church. He made it clear to Clare that he never intended doing so again. Brought up in a practising Church of Scotland family he was the victim of a very

authoritarian approach to God. Dragged along to tiresome
and seemingly irrelevant and lifeless services as a child
he had an image of Christianity which left him hostile
to anything spiritual. John tolerated Clare's Catholicism,
but deep down he resented Matthew and Rachel being
brought up Catholic. On Sunday mornings he would try
to sleep in while they went to Mass. He would lie awake
convincing himself that they were deluded and it was he
who was living in the real world. He loved his wife but
could not overcome his reservations about her Church.
Clare felt much the same about the Protestant
Church. Both found it hard to be open on matters of faith.

One snowy February morning while John was survey-
ing a site for a new office block, he had a telephone call
from the hospital. Clare had been involved in a serious
traffic accident. John's boss drove him to the hospital
immediately, but by the time he arrived, Clare was
already dead.

John was completely devastated and he had no idea
what to say to Matthew and Rachel. He knew he had to
be gentle but he also had to tell the truth. Out of love
for them and for Clare, he said mummy had gone to be
with Jesus, but the words meant nothing to him.

In the days that followed Clare's death all the conver-
sations he had had with her about Catholics, Protestants,
God and Jesus, echoed in his mind. His past sarcasm
became a source of guilt. His scepticism about life after
death diminished a little as his love for Clare made him
wish fervently that she be safe with God. He was also
tormented by the knowledge that Clare would have
wanted him to take Matthew and Rachel to church, but
he didn't know how to go about it. Finally he couldn't
stand it any longer and decided to see Father Tom, the
priest who had married them.

The comfortable priests' house, with its welcoming
atmosphere calmed John's nerves. It had a feeling of posi-
tiveness and hope about it. John shared with Father Tom
the story of how he had rejected Christianity and his
wife's Catholic faith. He told him all about the awful

tension in his marriage whenever 'faith' was mentioned. Now, he admitted, Clare's death and the children's future were making him ask fundamental questions.

Father Tom listened and heard all that John had said. 'I think if Jesus walked into this room now, he would understand and take you as you are, John', the priest said at last. John was shocked; he felt he should be being condemned, but instead he was getting off lightly. Does God really operate like this, or is there a catch somewhere, he wondered. Father Tom assured him that God does not try to trick us, but takes us where we are and leads us forward. With John's approval, Father Tom said a prayer. John could feel himself emptying of scepticism and being filled with a sense of wonder and awe. Father Tom prayed that John and the children would be given great courage and strength.

John could feel the tears welling up inside, but for the first time since Clare's death he felt hopeful.

Later, John shared what had happened with the children. He knew he didn't have all the answers but there was a new openness – the gap was being bridged. Why was it, John thought, that it had to take a tragedy to open his eyes to a simple journey that could have been made years ago?

◆━━━▶

My dear people,
let us love one another
since love comes from God
and everyone who loves is begotten by God and knows
*   God.*
Anyone who fails to love can never have known God,
because God is love.
God's love for us was revealed
when God sent into the world his only Son
so that we could have life through him;
this is the love I mean:
not our love for God,
but God's love for us when he sent his Son

to be the sacrifice that takes our sins away.
My dear people,
since God has loved us so much,
we too should love one another.
No one has ever seen God;
but as long as we love one another
God will live in us
and his love will be complete in us.

(1 John 4:7–12)

◄══════►

It could be argued that when two people meet and fall in love religious belief doesn't really matter. John and Clare loved each other but they came from different denominations and from a culture where that mattered. Did religion make a difference? Their story would seem to suggest that the answer was both yes and no.

The passage above gives us some helpful insights into the nature of God and love. What does it say to those of us who are involved in a 'mixed' marriage? It makes it clear first of all that we are all exhorted to love, 'since love comes from God'. There was love present in John and Clare's relationship, so God must have been in their relationship. If there is love there is God, so all those who genuinely love can take heart that God is in their midst.

If this is so, why was there tension present in the marriage when the issue of faith arose? Could it boil down to the fact that John loved his wife but not her God, or vice versa? Could it be that Clare had a deep faith and recognised Jesus as the source of life and love? It could be said that Clare had a friend in Jesus. Maybe John felt a little left out.

Maybe we can see an analogy with the case of two people having a drink of water: one is a plumber, while the other has no understanding of how piping works. Both enjoy the water but one has no knowledge as to how the water arrives at the tap; both drink and are nourished by the water but one knows nothing about its source. Should the plumber die, the other person must learn about the water supply to survive. In other words, it can take a crisis to call forth an openness and a desire to think and act differently. How often in a marriage does one partner not know the basics of housekeeping or finance until they are forced to deal with the problem?

In John's case, Clare's death raised within him all the questions he had been avoiding for such a long time. Questions like, Who is God anyway? Does it matter what denomination one belongs to? John had to confront these questions because he knew Clare would have wanted the children to be brought up as believing Christians.

Our Bible passage tells us that God's love was revealed to the world through Jesus. This belief was at the heart of Clare's faith. Christianity is not about denominations or lifeless services but about a person: Jesus. John had been brought up in a religious atmosphere but one in which the emphasis was on what he could achieve for God. Clare's death made him understand that it is not our love for God but God's love for us that matters. It was John's need for God that made him seek help from Father Tom. As we have said earlier, no amount of words or knowledge can convince anyone of the reality of God. Although Clare and John had talked, neither of them was open to the possibility of a shared faith. But when John met Father Tom he *was* receptive to the love that God wanted to share with him. He was still devastated and lonely; he still missed his wife; there was a vacuum that could not be filled – yet even in tragedy God could touch him. He was beginning to understand who the source, author and essence of real love is.

The divisions within Christianity can be aggravated by mutual intolerance in many areas of life. Nevertheless, although our unity has been impaired through separation, it has not been totally destroyed. We have all received the same love from God revealed in Jesus. We have all been baptised with the same Spirit. We all preach the same Christ.

Our dialogue has been hampered by our fears and often our cultural backgrounds. We often only converge when we are forced to reflect. John and Clare were not really aware of how much they owed each other and how much they held in common, namely love. When we recognise that the source of love is God personified in Jesus made man then we realise we have so much in common.

Jesus cuts a path through the darkness of guilt, doubt and even unbelief. John discovered it through loss. Is it possible that we can discover it through dialogue and mutual understanding?

FOR REFLECTION

1. Did the story of John and Clare strike a chord with you? Why?
2. Do you think that Christians should marry within their own faith? Denomination? Why?
3. What are the main difficulties in 'mixed' marriages? What part can the Church play in alleviating these difficulties?

PRAYER

Lord I pray that you will show me your love where I am. I thank you for the richness you show in all denominations. Help me to understand that you love everyone equally and you are interested in everyone. Give me an openness to hear and learn from others and the knowledge that you can reach me through them.

Why This Disability?

⊷

My STAY IN SCOTLAND was both productive and pleasant. When I had finished preaching in Glasgow I was due in Belfast. Some would say that now I was really going to an area where religious differences can lead to violence and bigotry. But all I could think was that I was going home to Northern Ireland.

I caught the ferry from Stranraer to Larne; in a few days I would be home in Donegal with my family. The revelry on the ferry was tremendous – people seemed to be in a party mood. Music rang out and the smell of good food caught my nostrils. In sharp contrast, however, to the happy atmosphere which prevailed aboard, I could see a young man curled up in an easy chair. The pain on his face was obvious, and occasionally I could see him tense in agony. He was in his thirties, tall, slim and athletic, yet as he got up his body seemed to tilt to one side. It was apparent that the only way he could find comfort was to walk with one hand behind his back. I watched him manage, with obvious discomfort, to purchase a cup of tea and carefully carry it back to his vacant seat. He was no more than a few feet away from me, and I decided to pull my chair closer. It wasn't long before we got talking.

The man's name was Hugh. He said he had been fortunate not to have been faced with many crises in his life. He was married with two healthy children and a secure career in teaching. He had had few things to complain about and even fewer worries. However, earlier in the year disaster struck. He developed a very painful and rare back complaint which forced him to have bed-rest. At first it didn't seem to be too serious but, gradually, it got worse. Hugh found himself unable to sleep and during the night he would break into a cold sweat as he worried about what was going to happen to him.

Hugh told me that he had always tried to be self-reliant and cope with whatever came along. He had previously enjoyed good health. Before middle-age managed to get a grip on him, he rediscovered the benefits of exercise and took up running. Gradually he came to love the freedom, enjoyment and sense of control over his body his new hobby gave him, and he found that he could run further and faster than he had ever achieved in his youth. He completed the London Marathon in 1989 and he thought that anything could be thrown at him and he would cope. Suddenly all of that changed overnight. He was completely immobilised and he felt he couldn't cope after all.

As the weeks went by it was obvious that there was not going to be any sudden change in his condition. His prayers became a process of bargaining with God. If you are supposed to be a God of love, why have you sent this condition to me? he asked. When his condition became worse still, he had to be admitted to hospital and put in traction for two weeks. Everyone at the hospital was helpful and kind and his neighbours and family came to see him frequently. He found great comfort in the attention that was being given him, yet the loneliness and the helplessness were extremely difficult. He had to forego so many things that in the past he had taken for granted: he had to stay in bed and was not even allowed to go to the toilet or wash himself. As he looked around him everyone looked busy and energetic and purposeful and it added to his pain.

Most of his fellow patients were in a more serious condition than he was so Hugh felt very guilty that all he could do was feel sorry for himself. He had been taught all his life not to express feelings and just to get on with things, so he tried to keep everything to himself. This meant that he was alone with his pain. Since he did not find it easy to express his worries and fears, nor to admit weakness, he had found an outlet in running, and in his work. While working and running he could usually sort things out in his mind without, as he saw it, 'burdening' other people. To tell others how he felt was running the risk of exposing himself, and he feared rejection. Maybe when people really knew him they would not like what they saw.

Now Hugh had no release. After a number of sleepless nights he felt himself sinking deeper and deeper into depression; he began to think that he was losing his mind as well as his body. In the middle of the night he picked up the Bible beside his bed. He hoped that it would remind him that God does not send any cross to us that we are incapable of carrying. All at once he realised he could not carry on with the pretence of being strong; he *was* weak and didn't care that people knew. His pride, had been beaten – he became aware of the frailty of human nature and was frightened. He needed help because he could no longer help himself. All he could do was cry.

The next day, the doctor told Hugh that he could go home while awaiting further tests. He felt like a child at the start of the holidays. At home he could get back to some semblance of normality and he would have the chance to tell others how he felt. He told me that admitting his weaknesses to God and to others did not take away the pain but somehow it lightened the burden. Complete physical recovery seems a long way off but at least now he is able to talk about it and is in a better frame of mind to cope. Eventually his pain will pass and Hugh said he hoped that he would emerge a better person. His condition has given him a better understanding of others in pain.

They then took charge of Jesus, and carrying his own

cross he went out of the city to the place of the skull or, as it was called in Hebrew, Golgotha, where they crucified him with two others, one on either side with Jesus in the middle.

(John 19:17–18)

Pain, as in Hugh's case, can be a personal crucifixion. Even in Jesus' case, although he had spoken many times about his death, when the time came he found it difficult to face. Despite his belief in resurrection the pain of crucifixion had to be experienced. Hugh knew that his pain would pass, yet he had to go through great suffering first.

The writers of the Bible are very cryptic about the crucifixion in comparison to the events leading up to it. The brevity is almost as if the writers could not bear to dwell upon it. St John, quoted above, was the only eye witness of the four evangelists. He saw everything take place, yet he adds nothing to the bald facts. He seems to long to hurry past it all. He says no more than he must, and almost distracts the reader by moving from the central figure, Jesus, to the minor figures of the 'two others'.

Tradition, history, art and meditation have all dwelt upon these simple words, and have tried to fathom them. They have brought the crucifixion forward as the hallmark of all that is best in human pain and endurance. The cross has become solace to the pain ridden, the poor and the down-trodden.

Hugh and I spent a little time discussing the terrible ordeal of death by crucifixion. Hugh's own suffering was obviously not as extreme as that, but he told me that he could identify with the pain that Jesus had to endure. He shared with me how he had been in the midst of many people but knew they could not understand how he felt. The crowds that gathered at the foot of the cross may have felt sorry for Jesus but they could not identify with the excruciating pain. Hugh, throughout his life had felt sorry for many others in pain yet did not really identify with suffering until he had to experience it himself.

Another person cannot enter into our pain. The best we can achieve is compassion and sympathy. Hugh felt the aloneness which bitterly brought him to his knees in depression. Jesus in his life had many occasions when circumstances tried to bring him down, but it was only at the crucifixion that the final consummation occurred. Hugh had obviously experienced little traumas in his life but all the time he had coped with them in the strength of his own being and thinking. His breaking point occurred in hospital. Jesus' occurred on Calvary. On Calvary, life had accomplished its worst, and Jesus was crucified not just in body but in emotions. Yet his strength and his resilience was apparent for everyone to see. Even his executioners declared it as they saw it showing through human weakness. If the life of Jesus can baffle us there is no question that his death draws the best out of us. In his death we can acknowledge the impossible. Hugh said that now he felt part of the tiny group on Calvary; he could stand as a result of his experience and truly identify with Jesus. He could now see, as Jesus saw, that pain and life are one.

Hugh said he could understand why the evangelists were so cryptic. When the years had passed and the truth of suffering had grown upon them, they understood that the only bland sentence to sum up the crucifixion was 'they crucified him'. When people have suffered in their own lives then this one statement becomes a reality which often defies further explanation. We, like Hugh, can only identify with real pain when we have been there.

FOR REFLECTION

1. Do you find it difficult to share yourself with others? Why?
2. Can you identify with Jesus' pain in the Crucifixion? How?
3. How do you cope with the aloneness that pain brings?

PRAYER

Lord Jesus, graciously hear the prayers which I make
when I am in despair. In your mercy lead me through
this day and night. Help me in my sickness so that I can
see some meaning in my illness.

Conclusion: Why Hope?

MY WORK IN IRELAND went well as did my precious time with my family. On my way back to our office I was pondering how to end this book with a message of real hope. A few months previously I had written a letter of sympathy to parents who had a 'still-born' baby. When I got back I found a little 'thank you' note from them. It read:

Many thanks, Pat, for your letter which we received after I came out of hospital. It's been a month before we could put pen to paper. The last month has probably been the hardest of our lives. We know that we had a daughter and we called her Ruth. The funeral was hard but it helped us to grieve and say 'goodbye'. It is hard to accept that life has to get back to normal and hard also not to resent that normality means living without Ruth. The pain has been beyond anything we have ever experienced. It is hard to see the hand of God in the death of a child that would have been so loved, so wanted and so important to us. We are sure that God will make some sense of it and give us peace when the pain of it all has subsided. We have had so many cards and callers. This lightened the burden somewhat when we knew that so many people cared. Their love and support carried us through. The whole tragedy has drawn us closer together as husband and wife. The future is a bit bleak and we are having to live one day at a time, but we

are getting there. Maybe in the future God will bless
us with children and we will appreciate them even
more as precious gifts, only lent, because of Ruth.
Well, Pat, it may have taken us a month to write,
but thank you for your part in holding us together.

As I read this note I felt that it summed up the transition
that exists in most of our lives between our pains,
whether they be emotional, physical, spiritual or mental,
and the search for hope. Pain can have many faces —
delinquency, alcoholism, mental illness, physical illness,
drug addiction, nervous breakdown, suicide and divorce,
to mention only a few. In the midst of the loneliness
which accompanies pain we all ask, Does anyone really
care? Does God care? I think love is the key to hope. The
first love that we experience is the love of others. God
can be so distant and remote, but the gentle hand of
loving people can display the love of God. The love of
God is our one true hope.

For myself I can only say that I am glad that I became
and have remained a Christian and a priest. As an evangelist it is always my privilege to share with people the
truth that God became man. We tend to see God as super-
human and not as the 'suffering servant'. It is always a
great source of comfort to people when the humanity of
Jesus and the people of the Bible are presented to them
in a real way, not a strictly religious one. God can touch
us in many different ways but especially in times of pain
and suffering. In our weakness we can experience the
great peace of God, and can go forward using our weakness as a stepping stone to change, development and
maturity. The only real mistake is one from which we
learn nothing.

In all our pain we must be patient with ourselves. We
learn slowly, and God is infinitely patient with us. The
trauma of being human can open the doors and windows
of our lives to God, and to others. We can waste such a
lot of effort in our lives trying to repress things and avoid
any unpleasantness, when pain can bring many aspects

of our hidden selves to the surface. The energy that is used in repression can be used constructively to help us grow and develop.

Suffering can also give us the ability to identify with those who are in turmoil. Jesus could not have spoken so powerfully to the world if he had not suffered. He has been there before us.

There cannot be real life without suffering. Suffering can make us and teach us to be human. These are not merely glib remarks: I make them as one who has suffered in my own life. All of us can have our own 'crucifixion'; it is how we deal with it that matters. We can become sour and negative or grapple with it, allowing God to touch it. The real test is whether, as a result of our experiences, we have a deeper and more meaningful contact with the people around us.

I feel sure that God can and does reach out to us in many ways. I think of the whole Bible as a simple written record of God in the lives of ordinary men and women, God permeating their experiences. I believe God wishes to speak to us. I believe that he has spoken to others – why not to us? Sometimes the only available channel of contact for him is through suffering. God wishes to be intimate with his own: he is no further away than his suffering people. We are *touched by love* through suffering, because suffering dealt with creatively yields strength.